Hun
and the
Wolf

Grace & Sage Simona

Teachings

Intro

Welcome, our Relation.

We are truly grateful that you have found your way here. Within the pages of this book, we will share with you, 7 Native-based Teachings, as we have learned and understand them at this point in our Journey. These Wisdoms: Humility, Honesty, Respect, Bravery, Wisdom, Truth, and Love come from the Grandfathers...those who have been since the beginning. These Teachings, while they are individual concepts, are meant to be lived simultaneously to the best of One's ability every day. To not live the Teaching itself, is to live its opposite.

Each of these Teachings is represented by one of our Relations from the Natural World, who emulate the qualities of the Teaching in who they are, and how they live their Life. It is important to understand the Teacher, so that the Teaching itself can be understood. While we will cover these Teachers and Teachings to some degree, True Understanding will only come if One seeks it far beyond this space we are now sharing.

You may have thought to your Self as you read the names of these Teachings, "I already know what these words mean", but do you really? They are not just words with a definition. They are a Way of Being, a Way of Life, and can be thought of as a Code of Conduct in which to govern your Self during your time here. To learn this New, Old Way of Being will take an enormous amount of effort and time on your part, and goes far beyond mere intellectual understanding. This is a life-long, life changing Journey. Your understanding will deepen and evolve over the course of time. You will go through many different versions of your Self, as the old falls away, to make room for the New. How you treat your Self, others, and view and interact with the World and all those you share it with, will profoundly change as well. Absolutely nothing will ever be the same.

Now, If One goes into this with a "know it all" mindset, then One will learn nothing at all. You must be willing and open to having everything you think you know, everything you believe to be True, challenged. Change cannot happen without change. To take and make this Journey will require endless work, trust, faith, sacrifice, selflessness, strength, courage, perseverance, fortitude, humility, surrender, forgiveness, and love to name but a few, on levels that cannot be fathomed, until you are there experiencing it for your Self. It will require you to face all aspects of your Self: Your shadow, your beauty, flaws, strengths, weaknesses, doubts, fears, insecurities, guilt, regrets (insert any word here). Nothing is off limits in terms of what you may be facing. Do so with courage, compassion, and with non-judgement of Self and others. Do it in the Spirit of Love, Acceptance and Radical Forgiveness of Self and others.

While we can never come close to capturing what your individual Journey is potentially going to look like for you, there are some common experiences and themes that are shared by those who walk this Road, which in all fairness and in the spirit of full transparency, you should know. This is, without a doubt, the most extreme journey that every One of "The One" will ever make. It is as brutal as it is beautiful. As daunting as it is rewarding, as painful as it is joyous. There will be many a time, particularly the times in which you are walking through the fires of transformation, that you will experience such intense pain, that you are sure, with a fair degree of certainty, that you will die from it, and in a way, you are, just not in the most literal sense. You must allow the death of your "old" Self, in order to make room for the "New" Self to be birthed. Fire is the great transformer, irrevocably changing all that it touches. It is best to learn to love it.

You are going to want to give up over and over, because you feel too beaten up, broken, and tired to continue. You will "think" that you cannot possibly keep doing this, but you can. Instead of giving up, give Thanks and keep going. You are stronger than you know, and it is only when you are pushed beyond your perceived limits, that you will find what you are truly capable of. We personally have wanted to give up more times than we can count, especially in the beginning and many times beyond that, but we never have and never will. At some point undefined, it is no longer an option to quit. This is an excellent place to be, because all that is left is moving forward. The quicker you can humble your Self and get comfortable being uncomfortable, the better off you will be.

What you are doing here is dismantling your Self. You are breaking your Self down to almost nothing, so that you can rebuild your Self in a better way. You are healing your Self on every level of your Being, and by doing this, you promote and facilitate the healing of others and ultimately the World in which we all Live. Know that it is within and through the struggle, that you will learn the most important of lessons. That it is within and through adversity, that Strength of Spirit is born. This is the way of the Warrior. So, when the Lessons of Life knock you down…get back up and give Thanks. And when everything that does not belong to you, and all that does not serve you, has been burned away…Give Thanks…And when you find Your Self on your knees, crying out for understanding…Give Thanks. And when All that remains, is the most vulnerable, authentic, raw and Truest version of You…weeping the tears of the Wolf…is when Understanding will come…Be sure to give Thanks.

Gratitude is a magnet for Miracles.

It is, we would say, critical to have support through this. Find others who are walking this Road. Form your tribe, your pack, your family, so to speak, and journey with them. Be each other's support, encouragement, and upliftment. Get to the place of selflessness individually and collectively, where if One falls, every "One" stops to help them back up, instead of leaving them behind. Where the pain of One, is the pain of All, just as the success of One, is the success of All, and the failure of One, is the failure of All.

Now, we do realize that much of what has been shared here could be a bit overwhelming, quite possibly, very overwhelming, but we do not want you to go into this thinking it is going to be easy, because it is not. We wish that we had known what we are sharing with you now, the many years ago, when we embarked on this journey for our Selves. We are not sure that knowing would have made anything easier, but at least we would have had some idea of what to expect. Without a doubt, the rewards, what is gained, far exceeds all the hardships endured. Given the opportunity to go back in time and make a different choice, we would make the same. We would still choose this Journey. We have been humbled to the core of our Being and as far as we have come, we know that we have that much further to go. While we love who we have become because of this and through this, we still have vast room for improvement. We are so grateful for all we have learned and understand, yet know that there is that much more to learn. We are in awe of the Strength of Spirit we have attained, but know that we will be made stronger or "Warriorized" further by each fire we walk through. Anything worth having must be worked for. It must be earned. It is just the way it is.

This is the Journey back to Your Self, or You, in your Truest form, as you were created and intended to be. Back to the place of innocence, where you just were and all else just was. Back to the time when the World was magical, and Miracles were a daily occurrence. It is a Journey of remembrance, the return to our origins, to Oneness, to Love.

We are so excited for you. May the Creator Bless your every step as you begin...The Journey...of a Lifetime.

We Humbly Dedicate this Work

<u>To the Creator</u>

We could not have done this

Without You.

<u>To our Earth Mother</u>

We are Grateful for your Love

And All that you give us.

<u>To All our Relations</u>

We are Honored

To share in the Circle of Life

With you.

<u>To Our Pack, Our Family</u>

Words can never express

The Gratitude we have

For each, and every One of you.

Prelude

It is best to actively Humble One's Self, than to be unwillingly Humbled. Humility is the foundation stone from which to build One's Self upon and is within its depths that understanding is born. It is an absolute requirement for One who has chosen to walk the Red Road.

One should be Honest with One's Self, with others, and in all of One's dealings. Honesty founded in Humility, provides the platform for One to not only admit when they are wrong, but also eliminates One from acting in prideful arrogance when they are right.

One should Respect All Life, no matter the form it takes. If Respect is founded in Humility, then One understands that they are no less, nor no more important than any of their Relations. One understands that Life is a gift, and that All Life is Sacred. We are guests here and are meant to be stewards and caretakers of our home and All who live here.

One must be Brave, Courageous and have the Strength of Spirit with them and within them, in order to make the Journey on the Road less traveled, which quite frankly, is undoubtedly the most extreme journey that every One, of The One, will ever make.

One should seek to obtain Wisdom and act with such. Wisdom is the fruit of knowledge and of lessons learned. Wisdom is not given; it must be sought, and it most definitely must be earned. Based in Humility, One understands that learning is an infinite process and is aware that in the vastness of All that is, that One knows close to nothing at all.

One should Live their Life in Truth. A Truth that they stand in, walk in, and carry with them wherever they may go.

Love...It is why you are here and what every One of The One is Created from and for. Honor the Gift of Life given you by the Creator and sustained by the Mother for All of your days.

Become a Hollow Bone
A'ho, Mitakuye Oyasin

Humility

It is in the depths of Humility

That Understanding is born

First Teaching: Humility

Humility is defined by Merriam-Webster Dictionary as:

Freedom from pride or arrogance. The quality or state of being humble.

One is egoless, modest and content, with the absence of any feelings of being better than others.

Oppositions to Humility are:

Pridefulness, conceit, vanity, arrogance, boastfulness, self-centeredness, self-glorification. Possessing feelings that you are better, more important, or superior to others.

Now, in the introduction, we mentioned that to not live a Teaching, is to live its opposite. This is the purpose of providing you, not only with the definition of each Teaching, but also its opposite. These can be used for the purpose of gauging where you are in terms of Living, or Embodying, the Teaching itself. It is important to be honest with your Self. This should not be about guilt, shame, or blame. You are not to beat your Self up over it, if you are to find that you have room for improvement. It should be an unbiased, nonjudgmental, honest assessment of where you are, so that you can identify where it is you want to be, and how you are going to get there.

The Teaching of **Humility** is represented by the Wolf, who lives not just for himself, but for the pack, the Family, or the collective of All. While all these Teachings are equally important, this one, by far, is our favorite. We personally consider this Teaching to be the most critical, because it is the foundation stone upon which all else is built.

To obtain a basic understanding of this Teaching, we must understand the Teacher, our Wolf family, and how they live.

Wolves live in a pack, which typically consists of 6 or more individuals, who are often, but not always, biologically related. The pack can be thought of as a family or a community. They are very sociable animals, with a strict social structure. The Alpha Male and Alpha Female "lead" the pack and are the only members (breeding pair) of the pack to have pups. As the leaders of the pack, they are accountable to, and for, the safety and wellbeing of everyone. They can be seen to possess the qualities of self-assurance, quiet strength, awareness, courageousness, selflessness, and those who lead by example.

The Alpha pair, as the leaders, shoulder the responsibility of All. Whether the pack is safe or has enough food to eat is dependent upon the leaders choosing a place to live that will meet All of their needs. Whether they eat or not is further dependent upon every member of the pack fulfilling their individual role in the hunt. Larger game, such as Elk, can only be taken down through a well-coordinated, collective effort from All, and minus, the very rare occasion, cannot be achieved by a single Wolf alone.

The other members of the Wolf pack, which may consist of generations of family members, each have their own role and function within the pack. All members take part in raising and teaching the pups about how to be a pack member and their place within it. As a pack/family, they do most everything together. They live together, sleep together, play together, raise the next generation together, and hunt together. They protect each other, love each other, and even mourn together when they experience the loss of a pack/family member.

So, what we have here in a nutshell, is a group of individuals who have come together as they are, in all their strengths and weaknesses, to work for and support something much bigger than just themselves. Something that could not be achieved by any One of them alone. These individuals, this family, works together in collaboration and cooperation, as opposed to in competition with and against each other. Their way of living is not about any one member being better than any other or what One did that another did not. It is about the collective effort of All, the success of All, and the survival of All.

Everything we have just talked about, in regards to our Wolf family, should be sounding quite familiar, because we have just basically described the social structure of Humanity, minus many missing key ingredients. It perhaps would be wise and in our own time, to reflect upon these things, so that we can ascertain where we have room for improvement both individually and collectively.

Now, if we take both the definition of Humility, its opposite, as well as what we know from the lives of our Wolf Relations, and apply them to the World in which we live, we must ask our Selves some questions.

Reflections

How can any One be an exemplary, successful leader, if One does not have the support and Respect of those they are supposed to be leading?

Do we have leaders who lead by example and what example are they setting?

Do we have leaders who are looking out for the best interests of All, or only themselves?

How can we achieve a state of unified and collective effort for the betterment of All, if we cannot do something as simple as work together?

Is it possible to stop making everything a competition?

Can we get over Our Selves, conquer our False Ego, our Pride, our Arrogance, our "know-it-all-ness", and our thoughts that we are better than, and superior to others?

Can we learn to be Selfless instead of Selfish?

Where did the need to be better than every One else stem from? Better yet, why do we support this way of Being with our participation?

Can we get to a place individually and collectively, where we are giving more than we take?

Can we stop diminishing and judging each other and instead act in such a way as to lift each other up?

Can we stop looking at our own and other's weaknesses as if we/they have somehow fallen short?

Is it possible to change our mindset so that it is focused on the strengths of every One, including our Selves?

Can we understand and accept that there is no possible way to know it All?

Can we be Humble and Courageous enough to embrace and fulfill our individual role here?

Can we learn to be of service to and for the betterment of All? Better yet, can we be of service, can we give of our

Selves and anything we may have, without expecting anything in return? This is Selflessness in its Truest form.

It is amazing and quite baffling to us, the numbers of People that we have crossed paths with, who think/feel that Humility is a bad or negative thing. That somehow it lessens you or weakens you. Humility is a Superpower in our book, and one of the greatest gifts and strengths that any One can possess. To know Humility is to understand your place within All that is, within the Circle of Life, and the Sacred Circle of Creation. It is understanding that you are a part of the Natural World, not separate from it and not superior to it. It is knowing that you are a part of something so much bigger than just your Self.

Now, quite often, the People of this World are unwillingly humbled by our Earth Mother in the form of catastrophic events such as hurricanes, earthquakes, floods, and fire, to name a few. These are wake-up calls, reminders to All of us of our place in this World. They are the ultimate reality check, the slap upside the head that tells us in no uncertain terms, that we are most definitely not in control here. Unfortunately, their effects are only temporary, and we can see repeatedly, within no time at all, that we go right back to doing exactly what we were doing before being brought to our knees. When will we ever learn?

Beyond being the Representative for Humility, our Wolf family teaches us about balance and the interconnectedness of All things, or The Web of Life. If we look at Wolf's part in the food web, we can see the connection between and among All living things, including our Selves. The food web itself, shows how energy is flowing or not flowing through an ecosystem, and how healthy or unhealthy the ecosystem is. In a word, this web is about Balance.

To conceptualize this Web:

Everything needs energy/food/a means to sustain its Self to survive. Let us start with plants. Plants sustain themselves from the soil, sun, water, and the insects who pollinate them. These plants are then eaten by any number of animals such as rabbits, deer, and elk, which sustains them. These Beings are in turn eaten by the Wolves, giving them Life, in addition to providing a means of population control. Any change, in any part of this web, will affect the rest of the web, creating an imbalance.

Humanity has discovered through the error of our ways just how true this is. By killing off the Wolves, other wildlife, such as deer, and their numbers, skyrocketed. With an exponential increase in the number of deer, land is overgrazed. Overgrazing can lead to soil compaction, loss of nutrients, a decreased ability to retain water, and erosion, all of which are big problems in and of themselves. Without enough food in the Natural World to sustain themselves, the deer turn to alternative food sources, such as the consumption of food crops, which ultimately impacts us. Nature is truly the compass we can look to when evaluating how healthy or unhealthy a state the World is in.

There is a balance that must exist between and among all living things. Our Ancestors understood this and lived Life accordingly. They harvested what they needed and no more. They were not wasteful. They did not pollute the air, land and water, slaughter animals by the thousands or chop down entire forests just because they could. They possessed a deep understanding of the land, those we share this World with, and the interconnectedness of All things. They understood "The Balance".

We are but one strand in the Web of Life, and what we do to any Being/any part of the web, we ultimately do to ourselves. So, when we pollute the land, the air, and the waters, we pollute ourselves. When we cut down entire forests, we take away the air we breathe. Until we understand and embrace this concept, we will not have the knowledge, the Wisdom, nor the ability to make sound, informed decisions that are of benefit to, and enhance the lives of, All who call this World their home.

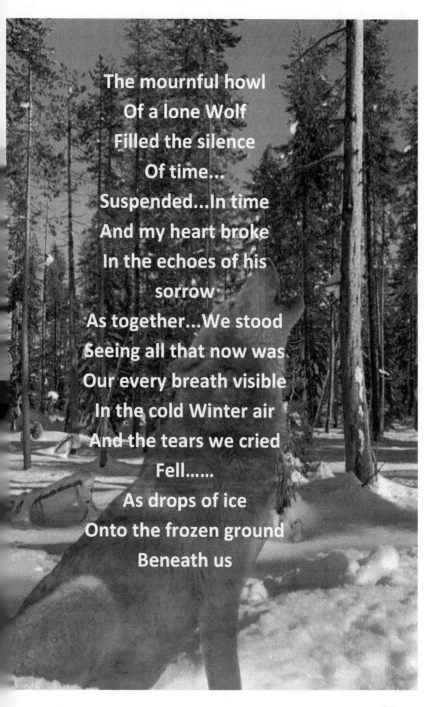

The mournful howl
Of a lone Wolf
Filled the silence
Of time...
Suspended...In time
And my heart broke
In the echoes of his
sorrow
As together...We stood
Seeing all that now was
Our every breath visible
In the cold Winter air
And the tears we cried
Fell......
As drops of ice
Onto the frozen ground
Beneath us

Honesty

It is within the depths of Humility

That Honesty is Born

Second Teaching: Honesty

Honesty is defined by Merriam-Webster Dictionary as:

Fairness and straightforwardness of conduct. Truthful, having integrity, the quality or state of being true or real.

One would be seen to be a person of their word, honest in all their dealings, devoted to the Truth, adhering to the highest principles and ideals.

Oppositions to Honesty are:

Deceitfulness, dishonesty, untruthfulness, characterized by deception or falsehood. Divergence from the truth. Hypocritical.

Integrity is defined by Merriam-Webster Dictionary as:

Firm adherence to a code of especially moral or artistic values. Incorruptibility. An unimpaired condition, being sound, the quality or state of being complete or undivided.

The Teaching of **Honesty** is represented by Raven because she understands who she is. She does not live life pretending to be something she is not, such as an Eagle or a Hawk. She honors herself by being true to who she is, in all her strengths and weaknesses, and by using her innate gifts to not only survive, but thrive. This is Honesty, and it is only when we are Honest with our Selves and others, that we can have Integrity.

What would an Honest person with Integrity look like utilizing the definitions provided?

This person knows their Self, in all their Strengths and weaknesses, and does not go through Life trying, nor pretending to be, someone they are not. They are Truthful with themselves and others, are Honest in all their dealings, and adhere to their values, principles or their "Code of Conduct" always. They are solid, unwavering, and incorruptible, no matter the circumstances. These People are the ones you can count on. The ones whose word can be taken to the bank. They are the "real deal", the "what you see is what you get" people.

What would a person look like who is NOT living in Honesty and with Integrity?

This type of person would have no idea who they are, and go through Life trying to be everything and everybody they are not. Who they are, or present them Selves to be, their principles, values, and way of "conducting" them Selves would alter, fluctuate or change depending upon the circumstances and people involved. These are the folks who have a lot of masks, meaning, who they are at work, home, in social gatherings, with friends, or with family are all a slightly, or possibly even a dramatically, different version of themselves.

Now, by definition, One who is not living in Truth, Honesty and with Integrity, would by default be living the opposites: deceitfulness, dishonesty, untruthfulness and deceptiveness.

Reflections

Does who you are, who you present your Self to be, alter or change, depending upon the situation, circumstances, or people involved?

Why is it, that we have such difficulty being who we really are? What are we afraid of?

Now, if we are to be True to our Self, we first need to figure out who that Person is, and this will require Honesty. We will need to be able to admit any number of things: That we do not know everything, that we are not good at many things, or that we are not as strong as we would like to be. At the same time, we need to be identifying our strengths, what we are good at, and what our talents and gifts are.

Can the level of Honesty that is needed for this assessment be achieved without Humility? The answer is No, and you will find this out for your Self. It is perhaps possible, to be this Honest with your Self, but Honesty goes beyond the Self. Honesty extends outward to others and is within all your interactions during your walk through this World.

Reflections

Is there any point to figuring out who you really are, if you do not Honor your Self by Living your Life in this Truth?

Does it not get exhausting, trying to be so many different people?

Do you ever have feelings of anger, that you cannot be who you know you are, and want to Be?

Would it not be a spectacular feeling, to be able to be who you are, and be accepted as such?

Participation in the Masquerade Party is NOT mandatory.

We will undoubtedly say this many times, "Humility is the Foundation Stone, from which to build your Self upon". We must be Humble enough to admit and accept all that we are and all that we are not. Humble enough to identify and accept both our strengths, as well as our weaknesses. Humble enough to know what we are capable of, as well as what we are not. Humble enough to admit when we are wrong, and not act in arrogance when we are right. Humble enough to Live our Truth, and not care what anyone else thinks.

There was a time - and it was not that long ago, when Honesty and Integrity were commonplace. These were the days when a person's word was as good as gold, and there was Honor in keeping your word. These verbal contracts were sealed with a handshake, as opposed to a legal contract 50 pages long, written in a language that nobody understands, for thousands of dollars.

The Truth of the matter is obvious. We each were Created to be unique, one-of-a-kind individuals. Only You can be You, and only I can be me. This World needs every One of us, as we were Created and intended to be. It is really that simple.

It is within the depths of Humility, that Honesty is born.

We stand together
As We are
In the space between
Neither here, nor there
Talking
Without speaking
Into the silence
Of nothing
And everything
No more
And no less
Then each other
Imperfectly, Perfect
Separate yet together
Two, but One

Respect

Life is a Gift, and All Life is Sacred

When this is Understood

Respected and Honored as such

The World will Change

Third Teaching: Respect

Respect is defined by Merriam-Webster Dictionary as:

To consider worthy. To hold in high esteem. To have concern for. To admire and appreciate. To hold in high consideration. To be in awe of or have reverence for. To honor.

One would be seen to be thoughtful and considerate of others. To have concern for others. To show appreciation for others. To hold others in high esteem. To treat others honorably.

Oppositions to Respect are:

Contempt, disrespect, to despise, scorn, ignore, disdain, dishonor.

The Teaching of **Respect** is represented by the Buffalo. Buffalo understands that we, Human Beings, have needs which must be met if we are to survive. Beyond understanding our needs, Buffalo honors them, by sacrificing his own Life and giving of every part of himself so that we may Live. It is important to understand that Buffalo does not do this because he is any less important than we. He does this out of Respect for All Life, and because he understands the balance that must exist between and among all Living things.

To Honor Creation, to Honor all Living things, is to have Respect.

Respect is a vast topic, so we are going to break it down into categories.

Respect for your Self.

A person who has Respect for their Self could be seen to exhibit love for their Self. They would care for, nurture and feed their Mind, Body, and Spirit, and consider themselves worthy of all that was good, uplifting, and in support of their highest and greatest good. They would understand, appreciate, and value their Self and live their Life in such a way as to Honor the Sacred Gift of Life they have been given.

Reflections

Do you Respect or disrespect your Self?

Do you consider your Self worthy? Worthy of Respect, Love, Happiness, and the Life you have been given, or do you feel for any number of reasons, that you do not deserve any of these things?

Do you treat your Self with care and concern?

Do you care for and Honor all aspects of your Being: Emotional, Intellectual, Physical, and Spiritual?

Key

Love is the Key, and it exists in All of these Teachings.

So, if we do not even like, much less Love, our Selves, how can we Respect our Selves? Care about our Selves? Honor our Selves?

Why do so many of us experience such self-loathing, such dissatisfaction, and a lack of Love for our Selves? Is this a Natural Way of Being or something we have learned, and if we have learned this, who or what was the Teacher?

Is the World we live in contributing to this? Is it facilitating Individuality or comparison? Cooperation or competition? Love or hate? Respect or contempt? Generosity or greed? Compassion or judgment?

Is any of this the way it is supposed to be, or just the way it has become?

Participation is voluntary, which means we can cease supporting this Way of Being any time that we so choose.

The Power of Choice is that we can always make a new one, a better one.

Respect for Others

One who has Respect for others would be seen as a caring and compassionate person. They would demonstrate thoughtfulness and concern for others. They would act with compassion and with consideration in their treatment of others. They would Honor, value and appreciate others for the Sacred Being that they are, as they are.

Reflections

Are you Respectful to others no matter their color, race, or status in Life, or do you find your Self in judgment of others? Ridiculing of others? Acting or speaking in ways that are disrespectful?

Do you walk by a homeless person on the street and think to your Self, "How disgusting! You deserve to be hungry and cold", or do you give them the sandwich you just bought?

Is how you treat others a reflection of how you treat your Self?

Treating others as you wish to be treated your Self, is Respect. To demonstrate Honor in all your dealings, is to have Respect.

Respect for our Earth Mother

One who Respects our Earth Mother would be seen as a caretaker of the soil, air, and waters and all those who live on and in them. They would act in, and with consideration of, the Earth's best interests and not just their own. They would appreciate, value, and Honor things as they are. They would take no more than they need, and give in return.

Reflections

Do we as a country and global community demonstrate Respect for our Home? What is the message that we are sending out in the form of litter and pollution?

Can we give of all we do not need to others, so that they do not go without? Can we repurpose instead of discarding and buying something new?

Are we only taking without giving back, and are our actions in alignment with Creation, or Destruction?

Are we practicing appropriate preservation and actively protecting All that is Sacred?

Giving of all that you do not need, is Respect.

Respect for Animals

One who Respects Animals would be seen as a caretaker of those they have taken responsibility for, and treat them the way they want to be treated them Selves. They would possess a deep understanding of the Sacredness of All Life and hunt with Honor, taking only what they need. They would express Gratitude for those whose Lives have been taken, and the Life this now gives them, in words or prayer, and by not being wasteful. This also applies to Plants, and any other Life form that we consume.

Reflections

Are we treating the Animals of this World, both domesticated and wild, the way we would want to be treated? Are we showing them love, care, concern, compassion, appreciation and Respect?

Are we wasting the food we have, wasting the Lives that have been taken so that we may eat? Isn't throwing any One's Life into the trash, the ultimate disrespect?

Can we understand that "food" does not come from the grocery store? Can we honor the fact that many are dying, that they are making the ultimate Sacrifice, that of their Lives, so that we may Live?

Honoring a Life taken with Gratitude, and not being wasteful, is Respect.

Life is a Gift, and All Life is Sacred. When this is Understood, Respected and Honored as such, the World will Change.

Buffalo Moon

Hold us gently

Through the long, dark nights

As we wait

For the kiss of the Sun

Whose touch will wake the World

From its slumber

Hold us steadfast and strong

In the Winds of Change

Whom blow with purposeful intention

And whose Voice

Will no longer Be Unheard

And as the snows fall

In unhurried silence

To land

In quiet contemplation

May we find reason

To give Gratitude

To Live, To Dance, To Laugh, To Love

In the Light of the Buffalo Moon

Bravery

Courage is born

When the understanding of One's destiny

The Life the Creator intended for You

Aligns itself with the Bravery required to Live this Life

Fourth Teaching: Bravery

Bravery is defined by Merriam-Webster Dictionary as:

The quality or state of having or showing mental or moral strength to face danger, fear, or difficulty. The quality or state of being brave.

One would be seen to be courageous, having "guts" or "a spine", having valor, resolve, conviction, and fortitude. Being fearless, heroic, determined, and resolute.

Oppositions to Bravery are:

Cowardice, fearfulness, weak, timid, meek, spineless, lacking conviction.

The Teaching of **Bravery** is represented by Bear because she has the courage to face her fear and make a stand. A Mother Bear defending her cubs, without a doubt, is a force to be reckoned with, and a prime example of both Bravery and Courage.

Now, to really get a grasp on what Momma Bear is doing here, we need to understand that she is typically fighting someone much bigger than she, and yet she does not run. Male Bear are a significant threat to cubs and if given the chance, will often kill and eat them. Despite the disparity in size, and despite the fact that she may be afraid, she stands her ground. She conquers her fear and will aggressively attack any male who gets too close, fighting to the death if need be, in defense of her cubs. She shows us, in her very way of Being, that no matter how peaceful we are as a rule, there are times when we must make a stand, hold our ground, conquer our fear, and fight for what it is that we hold dear, believe in, love, and care about.

Reflections

How do I, as a Being, compare to Momma Bear?

Am I fearful or Fearless?

What, if anything or anyone, am I willing to die for?

Am I a defender of the defenseless?

What am I willing to hold my ground and stand up for?

What do I care about, value and love enough to fight for?

These are immensely difficult questions that we should have answers for. Fear is a very real emotion that sometimes is warranted, and other times, not so much.

Fear can and should be conquered, as it does nothing more than hold us back from any number of things.

Reflections

What is it that you fear and why?

Do you fear being ridiculed?

Do you fear persecution?

Are you afraid of getting in "trouble"?

Are you afraid of failure?

Do you fear rejection?

Is your fear warranted or merely something you were taught to fear? And if you were taught to fear something, can you not unteach your Self, so that you can decide on your own?

Is it Death, you fear?

Let's talk about the uncomfortable topic of Death. Death, by far, seems to be the one thing that people fear the most, but why? Death is as much a part of Life as Birth. It is an inescapable Truth and yet, I can tell you in my 30 years of nursing, that I have witnessed hundreds of people do anything and everything to try to escape it. But Death always comes. Always.

Now, what would happen, how would your Life change, if you stopped fearing Death and instead befriended it and made it your Ally.

How many things would you do, that you will not do now, because you fear you may die in the act of doing them?

Would your answers to any of these questions change if you became Fearless?

What, if anything or anyone, am I willing to die for?

Am I a defender of the defenseless, or do I run the other way?

What am I willing to hold my ground and stand up for?

What do I care about, value, and love enough to fight for?

If we look to the past, there are many examples of people who lived their Life with great Bravery, despite the terrible odds they may have faced. They had Conviction. They stood up for what they believed in. Not only did they stand up for it, but they fought for it, and in many instances died for it.

To live your life in Truth, with Courage and without fear, is to know Bravery. To have Conviction in your decisions, to be True to yourself, and to stand up for what you believe in is Bravery.

Courage is born when the understanding of One's destiny, the Life the Creator intended for you, aligns itself with the Bravery required to Live this Life. In the hearts of those who possess this Courage, lives unwavering Faith, or complete Trust in the Creator always, no matter what. It takes far more Courage to be vulnerable than it does to be strong. These acts of vulnerability or great Courage come from the deepest parts of ourselves and can get us through the toughest, the most difficult, the most insurmountable odds of anything we may face.

Again, we have a lot to think about, and we would encourage you to reflect upon all these things, in your own time and at your own pace.

Tools for Your Journey

There are an endless number of things we can learn from Bear, beyond the Teaching of Bravery. These additional Teachings can be thought of as tools. Tools that can come in quite handy on your Journey, should you choose to utilize them.

If you have ever observed Bear, whether on a television program or in real life, she appears unhurried, as if she has the next 100 years to get where she is going. She is free from the concept of time and able to be completely present in every moment, whether this be strolling through the forest, tearing apart a log, jumping in the river, sleeping, eating or digging. This is reminiscent of the time we were children. Do you remember?

Do you remember what it was like to play? To climb a Tree, ride your bike, or splash in a mud puddle?

Do you remember what it felt like to go to bed and feel excited for the next day to come?

Do you remember wandering aimlessly through the World in wonder and amazement?

Do you remember when "Time" was as simple as, "It's time for dinner" or "Be home by dark"?

Bear's Courageousness is coupled with her childlike way of Being and her responsibilities are counterbalanced with play. She is showing us the need for balance in our Life, and reminding us that we are never too old, too "grown up" to have fun, play or be silly.

Reflections

Were we meant to lose our childlike way of Being just because we became "grown-ups"?

Were our Lives supposed to turn into endless amounts of work and responsibility?

Might we not all be happier if we had a Life balanced between the two?

Might we be missing out on our "Life" altogether because we don't have any "time" to enjoy it?

Does our current rushed, busy, appointment, deadline, and distraction driven World, facilitate joy, peace, contentment, relaxation, play, or balance?

How balanced are you among seriousness, responsibility, and fun?

How balanced is your Life between work and play?

Let's move on to the next set of Tools that Bear offers us.

One of the most interesting things that Bear does is hibernate. She may do this for several months out of the year because food is in such scarce supply. Prior to hibernation, especially in the fall, Bear will consume up to 90 pounds of food per day in order to store up the body fat she will need to survive hibernation. When it is time to hibernate, Bear crawls into her small, dark den, dug within the safety of our Earth Mother. Here she rests in the quiet, by her Self and with her Self, as she digests the prior year's experiences.

There are 3 key Teachings or Tools here: The power of silence, the need for alone time and the importance of reflection or introspection. While these 3 Tools are distinctly different, they work in tandem with, and in support of, each other.

Silence, stillness, and alone time are hard to come by in such a highly populated, overly busy, and noisy World. You may very well have to create a space for this or find one in the Natural World. We remember when we first started to sit in silence. It was extremely uncomfortable. Five minutes seemed to last five hours. Gradually, over time, and with practice, you will learn to still your Self, and embrace the silence. Eventually, it becomes not only easy, but enjoyable. The power that lies in the stillness of silence is phenomenal, and it is within the silence, that you will learn how to be alone with your Self, and enough for your Self, all by your Self. It is in accomplishing these things, that you will find the space that is needed and allows for introspection, or the process of looking within.

Introspection can be utilized to perform a Life Audit, or Life review of sorts. A process whereby you examine and evaluate, in Honesty, your Self and your Life. This process should be performed frequently.

Questions you might ask your Self.

Where am I in my Journey, and where do I ultimately want to be?

Am I living my Life in service to others, or only my Self?

Who am I right now? Do I love this version of my Self?

Am I living my Life in Honesty?

Am I respecting and honoring All Life?

In what areas of my Life do I feel inner happiness, and what areas of my Life have room for improvement?

Am I living my Life in fear or with Courage?

What or who in my Life is lifting me up, and what or who is holding me back?

Am I actively learning, obtaining knowledge, and seeking Wisdom?

Do I have a Truth of my own? One that I stand in, walk in, and Live in, at all times?

Am I acting in Love, and with Compassion?

Am I looking outside of my Self, to objects or people, to fulfill something lacking within me?

Why is this important?

Simple. If we are ever going to figure out who we are in our Truest form, if we are ever to heal our Selves and ultimately this World, we must do the work needed to achieve this, and these tools help us to do just that.

We are in a World that teaches us from a young age, the concepts of "who we need to be, what we need to achieve, what we need to look like, how much money we need to have, how we need to dress, the job we need to have, and the possessions we need to own" in order to be considered "acceptable, successful, or beautiful". It does not facilitate or advocate for individuality, and those who have the Courage to go against what society considers acceptable or "normal" are often ridiculed, exiled, rejected, and judged.

We need to be Brave and stop supporting this way of Life, this way of Being, with our participation. A house, car, degree, pretty clothes, an expensive pair of sneakers, and a bunch of money is not going to make us "ok", give us a sense of completeness, or provide us with real or lasting happiness. These are temporary fixes. A band aid on a severed carotid artery at best.

We must stop looking to the material world for our happiness, our identity, our sense of Self-worth, and completeness. We must cease placing the responsibility of these things on another's shoulders, whether it be a spouse, child, friend, or family member. Nothing outside of our Selves is going to bring us any of this. These things come from within, and it is our responsibility to provide them to our Selves.

What we are all searching for is quite simple, and has been there all along.

It is Our Self.

YOU, your True and Authentic Self, is what You are searching for.

Those who burn with the inner fire of Truth, Strength, Courage, Love, and the Knowledge of who they are, and what they are here for, are the People whose surety of purpose Changes the World.

One will never find

What it is

They are looking for

Outside of One's Self

All

That you are searching for

Is with you

And within you

Walk with Momma Bear

In strength

And with Courage

Journey to your Self

The Light

That Lives within You

Knows the way

Wisdom

Wisdom is not given

It must be sought

And it most definitely must be earned

Fifth Teaching: Wisdom

Wisdom is defined by Merriam-Webster Dictionary as:

Knowledge that is gained by having many experiences in Life. Understanding of what is proper and reasonable. Having good sense or judgment. The quality or state of being Wise.

One would be seen to be insightful, perceptive, discerning, astute, clearsighted, and knowledgeable.

Oppositions to Wisdom are:

Senselessness, preposterousness, illogical, unreasonable, foolish, ridiculous, lacking in insight and proper judgment.

The Teaching of **Wisdom** is represented by Beaver because he uses his innate gifts wisely and for the betterment of him Self, his family, and others.

Meaning of Innate.

Merriam-Webster defines it as:

Existing in, belonging to, or determined by factors present in an individual from birth.

Native, inborn, innate behavior.

Belonging to the essential nature of something, inherent.

To understand and put to work your own innate abilities for the betterment of yourself and others is to know Wisdom.

Beavers utilize their innate abilities, in a marvel of engineering genius, to construct their dams. They build their dams utilizing Natural Resources, such as mud, rocks, and the trees they cut down with their strong incisor teeth. These dams inhibit the flow of water out of the area, thereby creating a Beaver pond, or a deep-water refuge, which serves as protection against predators. Their home or lodge is constructed with the same Natural Resources utilized to build the dam. The bark, leaves, and twigs of the Trees procured to build both, additionally serve as a means of sustenance. Absolutely Brilliant.

We can see how the Beaver Family benefits from the use of their inherent gifts, but how does any of this benefit others?

Beaver is a Keystone species, which means they have an enormous impact on the Natural Environment, the way it functions, and are critical to maintaining its Balance. The ecosystems they create and inhabit are largely impactful to the Land, Trees, Plants, Fish, Birds, and a multitude of other Wildlife.

Beaver ponds benefit water Birds by increasing the area of open water, which provides more nesting sites. Trumpeter Swans and Canada Geese are two Bird species who largely depend upon Beaver ponds for their nesting habitat.

Beaver ponds are known to play a significant role in the water resources of arid and semi-arid regions. By damming the flow of water in the rainy season, groundwater tables rise, which provides areas with water in the dry season.

Beaver ponds have shown decreased amounts of pollutants and sediments, resulting in improved water quality in the areas they inhabit.

Beaver ponds also have a direct effect on both Trout and Salmon. Studies have shown that Salmon numbers are increased up to 90% in areas with Beaver ponds, as compared to those without.

Tree and Plant Life also benefit from Beaver ponds, by receiving a significant amount of water that was previously absent.

The Trees removed by Beaver thins out forested areas in a natural way, opens the canopy for more sunlight to enter, and creates space for lower growing Plants to flourish. This creates a more diverse habitat, which benefits a multitude of other Wildlife.

Their ponds can also serve as natural fire breaks, minimizing the spread of forest fires.

In knowing all of this, we believe we can safely conclude that the dams built by Beaver provide a sustainable, ecofriendly platform for change that benefits everyone, including us.

What we have here, in Human terms, is an Individual who utilizes their innate gifts/talents/superpowers wisely, and for the betterment of many. We have individuals who are giving back, exceedingly more than they take.

We are going to further pick this apart, so we can better understand how this applies to us individually and collectively.

For hundreds of years, Human Beings have changed or altered the Natural World, but has this been done with Wisdom? In the case of Beaver Dams and dams in general, we realized that we were lacking in both the knowledge and Wisdom needed to make these changes. As such, for the last 80 years or so, we have had to go back to our Teacher, Beaver, to learn a better way. Through them, we have begun to understand the interconnectedness of All things, the purpose behind everything being as it is, and the consequences involved when we do not Honor this. Beaver is now utilized and valued as a Natural means for stream and watershed restoration and in the prevention of erosion.

Reflections

Why is it that we, "Human Beings", think that we always know what is best?

Why is it, that much of our learning comes to us in the form of consequences, the unpleasant biproducts of our poor, uninformed decisions, and realized failures?

Can we come to the realization and understanding that not everything needs to be changed and that it is, as it is, for a reason?

Would it not be smart to obtain the knowledge base needed to implement change with Wisdom?

Might we want to perform a thorough evaluation of the desired change before we institute it? One in which we look at the potential impact it may have, both positive and negative. One that identifies the possible long and short-term consequences, for not only our Selves, but All living things, and the World in its totality?

Can we learn to institute change in an educated, thoughtful, ecofriendly, and sustainable way?

Innate Within

Each of us, like Beaver, came into this World, bearing our own unique, innate abilities and inherent gifts. Learning what these are, embracing them, and using them for the good of All is a much-overlooked part of our Selves.

This circles us back to Bear and the process of Introspection as a means of Self-discovery. It is through the discovery of Self, that you will also find your innate gifts or your Superpowers as we like to call them.

It is exceedingly important that each of us BE, who we came here to BE, and stop trying to be what and who we are not. We, just like each member of the Wolf pack, have a role within the collective of All that only we can fulfill.

If we look to the Natural World, we can see that everything and everyone is seemingly quite content Being what and who they are. Trees are not uprooting themselves to jump into the Ocean and become Whales, and Bears are not trying to fly. The Natural World and those who Live in it are by far the greatest Teachers of so many lessons.

Reflections

Why is it, that so many of us experience such dissatisfaction with our Selves and our Lives?

Why is it that we choose, in so many instances, to try to be like someone else instead of our Self?

Why are we constantly comparing our Selves to others?

Is "Rejection of Self" our Natural or Innate way of Being or is this something that we have learned, as a consequence of others, or Life?

Might it be Wise and of benefit to every One, that we stop buying into this way of being with our participation?

A Tool for your Journey

Beavers are a semi-aquatic mammal. They are excellent swimmers and highly equipped for their watery environment with large, webbed back feet, a paddle-shaped tail and a thick, insulating layer of fat. Beaver can stay submerged for up to 15 minutes. While under water, their ears and nostrils seal up and a special membrane covers their eyes, **which allows them to see beneath the surface with great clarity**.

This Tool teaches us to look beyond the surface of what appears to be real. To go deeper, or beneath the surface, so that we may obtain a clearer picture, a greater perception of the Truth of things. We can never dive too deep, ask too many questions, or obtain too much knowledge in the search for answers, and our quest for Truth.

Learning is an infinite process, and the path to knowledge. To understand the value of knowledge, to seek it, to cherish it, and to never stop learning is the road to Wisdom.

It was only when

I sat in the silence

that I was able to hear

It was only when

I closed my eyes

that I was able to see

With clarity

It was only in the stillness

that I became aware of my heart

beating in drum-like unison

with that of our Mother.

And it was in the clarity

of the stillness and the silence

that I understood

I was One

with All else.

Truth

Find your Truth

Live in it and carry it with You

Wherever You may go

Sixth Teaching: Truth

Truth is defined by Merriam-Webster Dictionary as:

A body of real things, events or facts. Actuality. A transcendent fundamental or spiritual reality. A judgement, proposition, or idea that is true or accepted as true. Sincerity in action, character and spoken word.

One would be seen to be truthful, honest, sincere, a person of their word, genuine, authentic.

Oppositions to Truth are:

Dishonest, insincere in action, character and spoken word, falsity, untruthful.

The Teaching of **Truth** is represented by Turtle because he carries the Teachings related to the beginning of Life, as well as the Truth of his own Life on his back.

To understand the Teaching of Truth, as it pertains to Turtle's Life specifically, we need to examine his shell. The top shell, or carapace, is made up of large, hard scales called scutes, and is attached to his spine and ribs, which unlike other vertebrates, lie outside of his body.

Turtle is born with 13 Natal scutes, which are found in the center of the shell. As Turtle grows, his shell must grow with him. This is accomplished by the growth of new and larger scutes beneath the ones he has outgrown. Scute replacement generally occurs once a year but can happen more frequently depending upon the conditions in which Turtle lives, and his growth.

A new growth ring appears on the outer edge of every scute each time they are replaced, and look like the growth rings that we find in Trees. The number of rings can serve as a rough indicator of Turtle's age, and the width of the rings indicate such things as times of abundance and growth, as well as times of scarcity, drought, and famine.

So, what are we seeing and learning here?

We have a Being, Turtle, whose shell, specifically the scutes and their rings, tell the Truth of his Life. They speak of how long he has lived and what he has experienced, good, bad, or indifferent during his walk through the Lessons of Life. As his shell belongs solely to him and is not detachable, his Truth too, belongs solely to him and is one that he lives in, walks in, and stands in, quite literally, every day of his Life.

Reflections

Do you have a Truth of your own and are you certain it is yours?

Do you Honor the Truth of your Life?

Do you always live, walk, and stand in your Truth, or does it waver or change depending upon the circumstances?

Your Truth/Belief System

Like Turtle, we each need to have a Truth of our own, one that belongs solely to us. Now, in order to figure out what our Truth is in terms of our own belief system, we need to put everything we currently believe to be True through a Truth test. This is a process of our own construction, in which we question absolutely everything. The purpose of this exercise is to weed out any "truths" we may be carrying that belong to someone else.

This is extremely important and necessary work, and you will most likely be quite surprised at the number of things found that do not belong to you and/or are no longer a "truth" for you.

Now, where did all this stuff come from? Everywhere, and it begins when we are small children, our most impressionable years, and when we have no knowledge base of our own. We are **taught** all kinds of things, by any number of people in our Lives. What really happened here, is that we were taught to believe what the people teaching us believed, which may or may not be a "truth" for us now. Then there is everything else: What we hear and see on the news, read in newspapers, books, magazines, on the internet and social media platforms, you name it. We are literally inundated with information, and need to be putting every last bit of it through our Truth test.

One of our favorite things to do, to stimulate people to think about what they are talking about and telling others, is to ask questions. These questions can be the same ones you ask your Self, when searching for Truth.

Our first question is, "Why do you believe this is True?" People answer in a variety of ways: I saw it on the news, I read it in the paper, I saw it on the internet, or my friend told me, to name a few. Our next question is the same, "Well, how do you know (what you read, saw, or heard) is True?" We typically receive a couple different responses from these questions, one being anger and the other being a look of bewilderment.

To blindly believe anything is just unwise.

The Truth of your Life

Beyond your personal Truth/Belief system, there is the Truth of your Life. Sometimes the Truth of your Life is difficult to bear. You may feel ashamed of it, embarrassed by it, weak and powerless because of it (insert any word you like here). Sometimes all that you want to do, is forget that any of it ever happened. We completely understand this, as we have had such Lives our Selves, and we will tell you, that it is not only possible to own all that you have been through, but also to value it. The moment we stopped being angry and feeling sorry for our Selves, and began to look at our Lives in terms of, "What have I learned? How have I grown and become stronger from these most unpleasant and difficult situations?" is when the game changed.

Absolutely everything, every situation, every Life Lesson, is an opportunity for Learning, Understanding, and Growth. When you change your mindset from this is happening to me, to this is happening for me, it changes your entire outlook and perception of the experience. Those who have had the most difficult of Journeys possess a unique skill set. One that gives them the ability to help people in ways that others cannot. A deeply wounded individual, who has gone through their own healing process, has the opportunity, should they choose to take it, to serve others in the role of a Wounded Healer. This is profoundly beautiful and sacred work, and a most honorable way to be in service to others.

It is when we choose to use our Lessons of Life, all that we have suffered and persevered through, to help others, that they cease to be a negative or bad thing, and instead become an empowerment for All.

The Truth of this World

Our World is kind of a hot mess, isn't it?

What have we done, or allowed to be done to our home?

How much longer are we going to allow this to happen?

Can we understand and take ownership of the fact, that we are the only species on the face of the Earth, who systematically and with intention destroys their own home?

Can we even begin to comprehend the ramifications of our actions or inaction as the case may be?

Isn't a lack of objection, nothing less than consent?

Is it possible to fix this giant mess we created?

How much more can we continue to take, without giving back in same?

Water is Life, we cannot live without it, so why are we polluting it?

Oxygen is Life, we cannot live without it, so why are we cutting down the Trees that provide this?

Have we been responsible stewards and caretakers of our home and all those who live here?

What kind of World are we leaving to our children and our grandchildren?

The state of this World, at a minimum, is overwhelming. Where and how do we start the process of fixing it? We would suggest that we start with the Truth. Until we can face, understand, and accept the Truth of what we have done, or have allowed to happen, because of our lack of objection, and the issues we face because of this, we cannot possibly move forward with the knowledge and Wisdom that will undoubtedly be needed to solve them.

A Tool for your Journey

Turtle is a cold-blooded reptile, whose body temperature is regulated through their environment. Turtle begins his day with the rise of the sun and spends most of it basking on logs and rocks to warm himself. Turtle requires an internal body temperature of 63-73 degrees Fahrenheit to be active, which is why basking both precedes and succeeds foraging in the water for food. When night falls, Turtle goes beneath the water to sleep, and will either burrow himself into the muddy bottom, or settle on a submerged object such as a rock or tree until sunrise the next day. Some Turtles hibernate through the winter depending upon where they live, and re-enter the World in the spring, when water temperatures reach the high 50s to low 60s Fahrenheit.

In terms of Turtle's Life, seasons and temperatures dictate the time for activity, foraging, breeding, and when to enter or exit hibernation. By living his Life in accordance with the timing of the Natural World, and patiently waiting for optimal conditions to exist, he facilitates ease in his Journey through Life.

This Teaching and Tool are an invitation to us to learn how to slow down and allow our Selves to become a part of, and a participant in, the Natural flow of Life. To learn that there is a right time for everything, and it is only time, when it is time. To learn to patiently wait for the opportune moment to present itself in the Natural flow of Life, instead of forcing our own agenda and concept of this.

Life is not a race, it is a marathon, and the Journey is as important as the destination.

It is only time when it is time
It is only rain when it falls
It is only hope when it calls
To the Heart of a land bleeding
And someone hears it

And what calls and is heard
Shall be saved by those that hear it
And with this deliverance
Will come deliverance

And what flies
Is free from the bondage of apathy
Able to soar and able to see in clarity
All that is visible and all that is not

And it is through grace
That grace will be given
While a heart that beats
That bleeds in Love
Will never Die

Love

Love

Is the most

Powerful Force that exists

And All exists

Because of Love

Seventh Teaching: Love

Love is defined by Merriam-Webster Dictionary as:

A strong affection for another, arising out of kinship or personal ties. Affection based on admiration, benevolence, or common interests. Warm attachment, enthusiasm, or devotion. Unselfish, loyal and benevolent, concern for the good of another. To hold dear.

One would be seen to be, Humble, Honest, Respectful, Brave, in possession of Wisdom, and One who walks in Truth. Devoted, appreciative, giving, caring, compassionate, loyal, unselfish, and concerned about others' wellbeing.

Oppositions to Love are:

Hatred, to loathe, detest. To show indifference to. To devalue, dislike, or show animosity toward. Neglect, apathy, disloyalty, unhappiness, ill will.

The Teaching of **Love** is represented by Eagle, who flies highest and closest to the Creator. Eagle carries All the Teachings because He is strong enough to do so, and He mirrors these Teachings back to us. Eagle's ability to soar high above the Earth allows him to see the Truth of all things, and all Ways of Being with great clarity. With his wings spread wide, He welcomes us in Love, **As We Are**, or to put it a different way, He welcomes us in Unconditional Love. It is when we can see our Selves as Eagle does, and Love our Selves as Eagle does, Unconditionally, that we are able to find Balance within our Selves, and extend this Love to others.

In Native Culture, both the Bald and Golden Eagle are considered to be the strongest, bravest, and highest flying of all birds. As such, Eagle is considered a symbol of Courage, Wisdom, Honor, Trust, Power, Freedom, Vision, Love, and Strength. He is the most Honored and Sacred of all Creatures, and believed to be both a Messenger of the Creator and the Carrier of the People's prayers to the Creator.

What is this telling Us? What are we to learn from this?

So many things.

This is about embodying and Living every Teaching that we have talked about.

It is the return to Unconditional Love, that which we were Created from and for, by "The One" who Created All.

Can we make the leap here, and see how Eagle, as a Messenger of the Creator, along with his ability to see, accept, welcome, and Love us as we are, is reflecting back to us, how the "Creator, God, Great Mystery, Source (All names of "The One" are welcome here)" sees, accepts, welcomes, and Unconditionally Loves Us, and is how we are to view and Love our Selves?

To get to the place of Love as taught by Eagle, we must Humble our Selves, so that we can in all Honesty, figure out, or remember, who we are. Who we were Created and intended to Be. We must have enough Respect for our Selves, to find, and Live in the Truth of who this is, with Courage and in Wisdom. It is in accomplishing these things, that we will find the "Balance" within our Selves that is needed, to Give Freely of these things to others, and Live our Lives, arms wide open, in Acceptance and Unconditional Love for All.

A Tool for your Journey

Beyond the Teaching of Love, Eagle, in his very Way of Being, teaches us the concept of duality. To understand this, we need to examine the many different and often opposing aspects that make him who he is.

Eagle is both a predator and a scavenger. A Being of the sky, as well as the Earth. His wings, while they are a pair and both are needed for him to fly, are split between the left and right sides of his body, in direct opposition to each other. If we look at Eagle's feathers, we can see that they too, are in colors that are the extreme opposite of each other. Some are dark in color, some are white, and others are both dark and white within the same feather, yet all are part of the same bird. What Eagle is showing us is the dual nature of himself. Ultimately, he is providing us with an example of the dual nature of Life and the dual nature of our Selves.

What is Duality?

Duality, simply put, is the existence of, and balanced interaction between two opposing forces. Examples include: Humility/arrogance, Honesty/deceit, Respect/disrespect, Bravery/cowardice, Wisdom/ignorance, Truth/untruth, Love/hate, white/black, hot/cold, happiness/sadness, up/down, beautiful/ugly, good/bad, left/right, or life/death. The list is virtually endless.

Understanding the concept of Duality can facilitate a deeper understanding of both Life, and our Selves, and supports both the content, and the statement made in the beginning of this book "That to not Live a Teaching, is to live its opposite".

When we can accept that Duality exists, realize that this is how our mind, in great part, makes sense of the "World and Life", and consolidate or unify these two opposing forces as belonging to the same entity, just as the left and right wing belong to the same bird, or as one emotion that has two extremes, is when we can begin to transcend, or overcome it.

In effect, what is happening here, is that we are obtaining an increased awareness of our Self, our thoughts (mind chatter), and emotions, and the resulting actions and reactions of such. With an increased awareness of Self, we can become more of an "observer" of our mind and start exercising control over "it", instead of "it" controlling us. This is the Journey of Self Mastery, and with Mastery of the Self, one is now in the position to make **conscious** choices and decisions, as opposed to acting, reacting, interacting, and speaking without thought or awareness.

Let us go back to the Teaching of Truth, and the example found in the **Truth of your Life** section. Here we talked about people who have had a difficult Life, which is more often, than not, described as having a "bad" Life. Utilizing the concept of Duality, we know that if "bad" exists, then its opposite, "good" must also exist.

Is it a Natural process for us to look for the "good" in a "bad" situation, or are we more prone to keeping our focus on the "bad"?

This is where Self Awareness and Self Mastery come into play.

Utilizing this example, we became "aware" that our mind was focused on the "bad" of the situation. Now that we are "aware" and have become an "observer" of our mind and its thoughts, we can make a **conscious** choice to change our perception and look for the "good" in the same situation. In this case, we chose to look for what we had learned, how we became stronger because of it, and how we could use all this moving forward for the betterment of not only our Selves, but others. In doing this, we thereby created a "balanced" interaction between these two opposing forces. Another way to think about this, is that we have attained a State of Neutrality.

This is such an important concept to understand and incorporate into your Way of Being. It quite literally can and will change, if you allow it to, your perception of every experience.

The many facets of Love

Love has multiple facets to it, many of which are overlooked. It is so much more than the "mushy, gushy" emotions that it is so often associated with. So let us look at some of the not so obvious, but exceedingly important, facets of Love.

Love is making sacrifices for the betterment of others. It is a Champion of hard work in the fight for a cause, or on behalf of another who cannot fight for themselves. It is Courageous and Brave in its defense of the defenseless. It is extending a helping hand to lift others up. It is fierce in its protection of those who cannot protect themselves, and of All that is Sacred. It is Compassionate in its witness to the suffering and atrocities of this World. It is resolute and steadfast, in both the good times and the bad. It is Selfless in its giving and generosity to others, expecting nothing in return. It is nurturing in its care of others. It is the tears that fall when someone passes, or begins a new

Journey, and in its most extreme manifestation, it is giving your Life for another. All this, and we are sure there is more, along with all the "feel good stuff", is Love, and it is this kind of Love, in its totality, that will change, even alter, the trajectory of this World.

Writing this book has indeed been a labor of Love for us. We have laughed, as much as we have agonized, in its Creation. So much of what we have spoken about, or written within these pages, literally manifested into our reality as we wrote. While writing about Humility and the Wolf, One of our pack fell down, and as it was written, every One else stopped and helped them back up. Our lives were inundated with people, masquerading as someone they were not, during the Teaching of Raven. We felt that we had quite literally been trampled by a herd of Buffalo, in the writing of Respect. Our Courageous Momma Bear took us into hibernation with her, where we journeyed within our Selves. Beaver very nicely reminded us of all that we do not know, and how much more there is to learn. Turtle, in True form, slowed us down to a crawl at best, to be sure, we are guessing, that we enjoyed this Journey. In the end, Eagle came down and embraced us in Unconditional Love, for who we are, as we are. Such an overwhelmingly, beautiful experience.

We now freely give to you all that we have learned, in Love and with Love, for who you are, as you are. May it serve you well on your Journey back to your Self, back to Oneness, and ultimately back to Love, that which you were Created from and for, and are intended to Be.

Abundant Blessings to you.

Grace & Sage

My Love for you

Reached out
To bridge

the space
Between us

To my eyes
You appeared
So different than I

But when I touched you
My Heart
Revealed the Truth
We are One

Outro
Prayer for Humanity

May we choose to be Humble, as is our Brother Wolf, who lives his Life in selflessness, in cooperation with and in service to and for, the survival, betterment and success of All. May we understand the value of Honesty as taught by Raven who lives her live in such a way as to be true to herself. May we learn to be honest with ourselves, with others and in All our dealings as we walk through this World. May Buffalo gift us with the understanding of what it means to sacrifice and give of ourselves from a place of Respect, Understanding, Compassion, Love, and in the Spirit of True generosity. May Bear give us the Courage we need to walk the Red Road and face our fears, so that we fear no more. Courage is born when the understanding of Ones' destiny, the Life the Creator intended for you aligns itself with the Bravery required to live this Life. May she help us to understand the strength of solitude and the power of silence, as we go within ourselves in search of the answers we seek. May Beaver give us the Wisdom needed to interact with this World and All living things in ways that are sustainable and of benefit to All. May Turtle help us to slow down so that we may enjoy our journey here and the Life we have been given. May he gift us the ability to find our own Truth, so that we may Live, Stand and Walk in Truth wherever we may go, just as he. May we learn to use the Lessons of Life in ways that serve both ourselves and others. May Eagle teach us to soar on the winds of change and give us the sight to see All ways of being, with clarity and Truth. May the Tree People give us the strength to stand strong through adversity. May our Mother teach us what true compassion and unconditional Love is, as she holds us in both. May Great Spirit instill in us the ability to Forgive so that we may free ourselves from the past, which exists not for us to live in, but to learn from, so that we can move forward in a better way. May we learn well. Great Spirit guide our every step and Bless us ALL.

A'ho

Contact Information

Please feel free to contact us with any questions you may have, or if you just need someone to talk to as you Journey.

Unitedspiritwolfhealing @ gmail.com

Be Well, Be Strong, Be Courageous, Be Love

Grace & Sage

Walk softly upon our Mother

Each step

But a whisper in the wind

Walk gently

In Humility and Gratitude

For the Breath of Life

You have been given

Walk with Courage Sacred Warriors

as you travel the Red Road

Always standing in your Truth

Walk in Reverence, Respect and Love

Of All that is

In the Wisdom

That All life is Connected and Sacred

Walk in Beauty

This Book can be found on Amazon.

Made in the USA
Middletown, DE
14 May 2021